# the Chronic Period

**Also by Latif Askia Ba**

*The Machine Code of a Bleeding Moon*

**Series Editor**

Chris Martin

**Cover Description**

The cover features a bright yellow background with the title rendered in hand-lettered red cursive type punctuated by disruption so that a continuous line is suggested while being intentionally broken apart. The subtitle is set in black in a continuous line that bleeds across both sides of the cover, and the author's name is set in green hand-lettered capitals that are also marked by interruption and dance across the page to suggest unique, joyful motion.

# the Chronic Period

poems

LATIF ASKIA BA

MILKWEED EDITIONS

(800) 520-6455
milkweed.org

Published 2025 by Milkweed Editions
Printed in Canada
Cover design by Mary Austin Speaker
Author photo by Tarek Dekkaki
25 26 27 28 29 5 4 3 2 1
*First Edition*

Library of Congress Cataloging-in-Publication Data

Names: Ba, Latif Askia, author.
Title: The choreic period : poems / Latif Askia Ba.
Description: First edition. | Minneapolis, Minnesota : Milkweed Editions, 2025. | Series: Multiverse | Summary: "A ground-breaking collection of poems exploring disability, syntax, and rhythm from a Brooklyn-based Senegalese American writer with cerebral palsy"-- Provided by publisher.
Identifiers: LCCN 2024017265 (print) | LCCN 2024017266 (ebook) | ISBN 9781639551187 (trade paperback ; acid-free paper) | ISBN 9781639551194 (ebook)
Subjects: LCGFT: Poetry.
Classification: LCC PS3602.A18 C48 2025 (print) | LCC PS3602.A18 (ebook) | DDC 811/.6--dc23/eng/20240418
LC record available at https://lccn.loc.gov/2024017265
LC ebook record available at https://lccn.loc.gov/2024017266

Milkweed Editions is committed to ecological stewardship. We strive to align our book production practices with this principle, and to reduce the impact of our operations in the environment. We are a member of the Green Press Initiative, a nonprofit coalition of publishers, manufacturers, and authors working to protect the world's endangered forests and conserve natural resources. *The Choreic Period* was printed on acid-free 100% postconsumer-waste paper by Friesens Corporation.

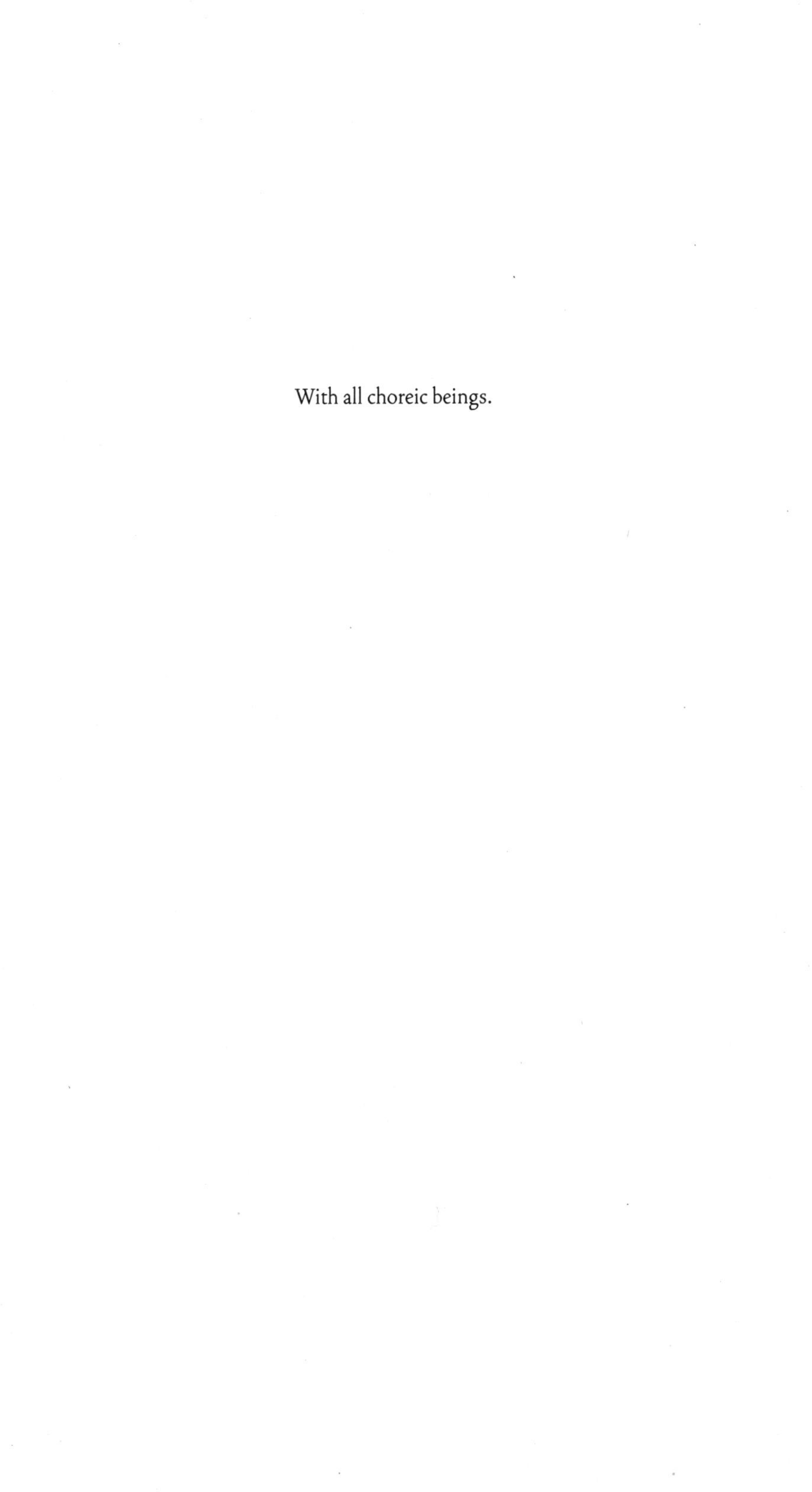

With all choreic beings.

# Contents

# the Chronic Period

# Choreic

I put a period in the middle of your sentence.

I put a period in the middle of your sidewalk.

I put a period in the middle of your gaze.

I put a period in the middle of your bodyhood.

What is the most obvious thing about me. Tell me so that I know.

I want you. To say it because

in poetry we won't say it. In poetry. We can't say it. In poetry

we don't want to say it. We say no.

No no no. No. Don't say the thing.

Don't say the thing. Never

say the thing. I put a period

in the middle of the thing. I put

a period in the middle of your disability.

So that now. When I breathe

you. Are trapped in my breath.

So that now when I speak. You

take refuge under my tongue.

So that now when I. Dance you

quake. In the dyskinetic

void of your abdomen.

Every time I lay to encounter you. It becomes clearer I must eventually. Abandon my disability. What exactly is my disability. I don't know. The institutions have called it different things at different times. All under. The name of cerebral palsy. We bow now to the name.

It was easier to bow when I was shorter. Nowadays I am taller and much more. Difficult. Basal ganglia where are you. I'm tapping on the root of my skull so that I can distill. Your silvering metamorphosis. Oh. You wanted English so that's what you're getting. Silly silly alpha. Bigging up himself so that his chest is the wine-pressed helm of a Greek letter. He doesn't know his marble calf is a burgeoning. Neocolony.

Looking down at my shining scoliosis I'm reminded. Of my Yemeni physical therapist pushing her narrow fingers. Into my left side. The world. Is big and round on a therapy ball and you want to be pretty and stay on forever. You want to straighten and. Straighten. And straighten. So that every bone stretches into one undiscovered image.

# At Stop & Shop

Through the storm
there was an elusive starring. A red
anyway. Somewhere on Atlantic
and 4th. You said
there was too much money
on my food stamp card.
That is shopping.
Waiting and waiting
and beeping. Dawn stops
for a moment. Fi ñaam
her muffin. Regarding disability
there are almost too many syllables.
Such a simple thing. That I
am not my body. But
the inside
of a seed.

# Syntax

So the kid can walk. But not good. He can walk but only
at the ends of your fingers. He can walk but he leaks. You have to

change his bandanna after lunch. He can walk but his bandanna
is leaking. He's opening his mouth now. To say something. He leans

to the right. Hold his hand. He's talking to you. Tell him to swallow.
He's saying something else now. Tell him to say it again. He's leaking

again. They always pack him an extra bandanna. Each color for the color
of his leaking. Around his neck. He walks. Leaning curiously to one side.

Holding onto the banister. Tell him to say it again. Open his snack. He can
feed himself. With his right hand. If it drops. Tell him to try again.

# 5 juillet

Dear Xadi

Moving back and forth
from the window
to the bed. Trying to become
the space in between.

To define this space
I'll try to translate it.
By moving very slowly.

Noting each item.
From the window
to the desk. I walk away
toward down
across.

I have taken out all the unnecessary
adverbs. Adjectives. And any other
approaching quality
so that whatever
is left.

You struggle with. I feel
sort of guilty about the vodka
and ice on my desk. Constantly
getting ready for my 2 a.m. Birth.

When you put it like that. The poem
is a filtration mechanism. Into which
I shove my head. And scream.

When you put it like this. The space
we had discussed earlier. Enters
again.

## 3 octobre

Yes. The disability
is slow. Unlike the bachata
in which we grew. Accustomed.
One letter at a time. Ay
padre
ay coño. Ayayay as I thrust myself
into the shower stall. Unsurprised
again. By the brutish calculus
of the body. Mah pacá. She moves
the chair forward and puts
on the brake. How to measure
the silence
of this. 22 milligrams. 6 microondas. 1
microorganism in which
you dance as you cook.
Vivo trabajaaaando. She sings
very plainly.

# 8 juillet

Dear Xadi

This is the feeling I was telling you about. Unnamed.
Unenamored. Like putting your

right cheek against a sheet of rose petals. I don't know
what to say. I don't want to do anything. I don't want to consume

anymore. I want to devour. Food has always been a point
of slight contention. Like a tightened joint. Like my left knee

never quite. Extending. Never
quite knee. I water my joints.

I would ask you to roll me one.
The left one. The knee. So that we can get high

and remember. How to describe
the body. Here is the feeling I was telling you about.

# 28 avril

In doing this we become more like him.
Which isn't much of anything.

Our hands like beetles curve into
form. Hmm much better. He will hum

along like this. Clasping his right wrist
with his left hand. It's a wonder how

he gets his pants on every morning.
One bevel at a time. It's almost

underwhelming. Once he took the stage.
After each poem he read. His professor

would read it over so the audience
wouldn't miss anything. He gave

his permission of course. He gives
his permission to anyone who asks.

Here he comes now. Spelunking. Just ask.
He'll answer. Here's the cup of water

you've placed me in. I have finally become
a straw. He nods enthusiastically.

# 20 janvier

Inching along
pushing along. Some
uncomplicated blue.

My battery fortified in my metallic bowels.

Or had the manufacturer fashioned
my cushions. For some simple violence.

The screeching of fresh duct tape. My metal feet
are becoming round again.

On breaking myself. My small wheel got stuck
between the train and the platform.
There was nothing else to say.

My glorious return to formlessness.

## Djabote

Cheikh.
Cheikh.
Cheikh.

This ardo isn't waiting for anyone to tell him where to shit.
He's forgetting how to distinguish himself from his throbbing sabar.
From the foghorn he heard blow.
Here comes the golo now. He circles himself with his hands. Over
out. Out. Over. Over out hand. Drop. So that the palm in the center
be the lowest pitch. The period. He laughs.
Who is sitting outside the hut now.

Eigner or some sort. Of twisted Yiddish Patwah. Some sort of obeah. Or that césairienne hour where gorée snaps off any thing. Hung. Ear ear ear. Dégg. He know how fi riddim himself. Jàpping incessantly. He drums himself into the conducted quiet.

Like this. He answers
the silence. The in between
Being wholly enough. He answers
bu jigèèn. To address his wombic qualities.

The white woman tells him his translation
                    is minstrelesque. Jox ma jox ma
jox ma.
He thought at first.                    She said something else
which would have made for                    a prettier word.

This is the history he can't remember. The one he is constructing from the sand-straddled glossary of his mother tongue. Disspeaking. He licks the wall with his eyes. Red. Cris du gaynde. Jooyu N'Diaye. The center being the only thing.

He doesn't even want to be ci jamm. He wants the want to open
the distended ear or his tam tam. The stick
being a perfect appropriation of his sound.          The one he uses.
To stir          his toes. Out of their stoic retrogression.
His     being a long dance          no man has dared answer.

Here comes the spindrifted sun
through the open accessaride window. Drugless. He is.
Spotless he. Is
shitstain light. Smiling spine and
this chant he doesn't know.
The crying was sweeter if it had been longer deeper
and more alone. But this is just him.
Jàpping again.
Yellow.

Not sure if that's him singing or his liable eardrum. The clerk keeps directing her speech to the nearest able body. This must be frustrating he thinks to himself holding in the montage of the Pakistani paysage his eye so hungry locus. Ma'a salama he says like a wolf.

Flat hand center. Open. Or tenacious.
He cups the air in a slap that curves and turns electric.
Nuyul ma sa yaay if you're going in that direction.

Listening. His world is on the underside
of his belly. Though this large western village
keeps trying to tell him he's not.
He is.

Taking his naps in his left hand rake.
What is it you wanted tell him.
Xam naa.                He answers. His beautiful poulo neck.

He doesn't want peace. He wants you to shut your bec for a second. In this way he can hear the entire anglophonic lie. Each language he has devoured he pukes up his mother holding. The bin under his trembling chin. His inner neene. Backsplashing.

Open. Flat. Center. He moves
in the direction of his undoing. The leg his angle.
His tool the foot. The ear not for dégg
but àgg. Or his very own positioning.
Please wait so that he can. The Eigner in him
is already unbearable. He strokes the drum
faster. The horn of the shored guineaman.

# 22 septembre

In the six o'clock evening. I am waiting
outsidesun. Someday my prince. Inflected.
The man lifts me. With a crank. Into
the accessaride. A brand new room. Full
of sitting down.
Sometime in college
I started reading
myself. In beautiful compiler code.
Hooking my chair into place. In case
we flipover. I can dangle from the roof.
Like a monkey. I watch
as he takes three dollars
out of my wallet.
He counts each
one out loud.

# 28 septembre

Night. Carve out some space
for me. In trying to say

nicer things. The black sky
says nothing back. As usual.

I'll try to stop you tomorrow
and mouth your name

never before heard
in my beautiful accent.

Palsied. Not
quite right.

Palsied
is not quite right.

# 9 août

Dear Xadi

It's not depression. But something
a little more orange. That I lie

in bed naked. Before turning off the music
in order to realize. How tired I am.

Of what Xadi.

I think I'm headed in the right direction
when I wake up and put my clothes on.

When I wake up. And open the shade.

The people out there. Say they love me.
But none of it uncomplicates

the way I saw myself in the mirror today.
My pink shorts. All bunched up like that.

It's not self-hatred. But another color.
Thin and fast. Almost incroyable.

She started to cry. In front of a pizzeria
on 5th Avenue. She wasn't sad.

She had just finished explaining something
to me.

She had explained it perfectly.

# Alegre

This is a class allegory. The adults open their mouths and make sounds
that signify nothing. Am I first generation. Or nonordinal. My father's voice
in between these strange bouts of cold. T'as coupé le son.
It sort of helps. But looking out my window I'd rather just be the cat
catching sun in your garden. You speak into my left ear. I rearrange you
accordingly. Suppose the word was the point. At which sound touched
meaning. I'd press my hand to everything just to hear. Your tangent
lines. Suppose my broken gait was a word.

# Douglass Pool

Pulling my left shin
into my chest. Like this.

I wonder if this lifeguard
thinks I'm a freak. In water

limbs are even more
like antennas. The first thing

I do
is go under.
To prove to myself

that the body can. Be completely
surrounded.

Remembering water
is like remembering your
iridescent thighs. In this instance

you is just another pronoun. Like
when she said you can go through
the woman's side. As if to say
you and your body

are not a threat to women. Or
the sex of your aide will determine
your species. Though in water

I push in all the regular ways.

She says I'm not allowed to wear
my purple shirt. White shirts only.

So I imagine myself completely
as leg. Curling around
the perimeter of my reflection.

This way. My body looks
like a dancing tattoo.

I never had intended
on wearing a shirt.

# 9 novembre

Omar is bumping three 6 mafia in the living room and it is not unlike being a kid and climbing onto the scottish man's back and him taking me and throwing me back into the water. Being disabled is okay if someone is throwing you back into the water. The sun is feeling herself today and this has nothing to do with me firing my aide last night. She been played herself which has nothing to do with anything especially not horses and how when they shit you can feel their bowels vibrating underneath you which I find kind of endearing. And there is always a dubplate spinning in my room and this is completely on accident and edinboro which sounds like edinburgh when I say it so I have to say no. Not scotland but nowhere all that interesting where one old van driver referred to the town as a frozen hell. Edinboro needed reggae very badly unlike mark who downed a handle of bottomshelf vodka and drove on the icy roads at the crack of ass. Hung completely over. He brushed my teeth laughing and sold poems. This had nothing to do with mark from england who asked if I was happy and I said yeah I'm good and he said I was always happy and turned the lights off.

## 5 mars

Il commence avec infirmité et silence. Yellow chapeau. Though not quite.

He knows it takes discipline. But he refuses to tell you.

Rest of the time he's confused about simple          day to day things.
Location time positioning the conundrums of prepositional       phrases.

Shapes. Yellow        being the beginning
of the month. Of the mouth he is opening. Some obtuse
angle       and a janky isosceles.

He rearranges his desire from the wisdom of his stomach.

Being          the only way to distinguish himself. Does he
really need this he asks          pressing his forehead
into the back of his wrists.

The calculation requiring a warmer more meticulous instrument

he offers you his right arm.

# At Stop & Shop

Two ripe plátanos. Two green.
There's no dark place

in a supermarket. The plastic wrappings
longing flesh. I asked Dawn

if she had to search fi cord.
She said yes. But ya na come back

wid it. I swallow a fistful of white rice.
I imagine living in a clay pueblo

slow. Anesthetized. Please enter
your PIN. I tell it to you now.

My queering consonance. Rendered
by your fingers.

You type me in slowly.
Each digit. A psalm.

# 7 avril

This Upanishad. Says something
about karmaless doing. Doingless
action. Or pouring ataaya
from very high above.

Mom cuts the potatoes into 1/4 inch slices.
She gets a ruler to prove it.
Before whisking

there's a thin moment.
She's yours.

# Syntax

It took him a while to eat last night. She told him he shouldn't talk when he eats. Just chew. He doesn't think he's chewing properly. He thinks. Things are getting rather ambiguous and this reminds him to call Medicaid. Especially ambiguous. He sits on the futon like he sits on the toilet. Not quite waiting not quite ready not quite at all. He sits in. His chair and tries to be very still and the doctor holds his hand and asks him if she makes him nervous which he finds sort of sweet and embarrassing. He lies down on his belly he lies down on his back he lies on his side. He's slightly worried about the intricacies of speaking. That each time someone asks him to repeat himself. The thing being repeated dies a little. On the other hand. Some people don't understand him and don't ask him anything which is just. As good as killing him.

# 12 février

There's a pimple on my right ass cheek. But I have no one
to show it to. Sandra might see it

when I climb dastardly. Into the shower. But that's not showing.
Showing calls for a general orientation and an off-red.

Almost a bërëb. At camp I still remember the mysterious
angles. Of the bodies. Cattywampus as they were lifted wrung

draped and chaired. Ready for senate. How it felt
when I was a kid. Emerging from the shower. Slipping past

mom. I'd prance up and down the hallway. In a color
unmatched ever since.

# 3 juillet

Twenty minutes up the road

her family hills flowers

and pound cake

folks

like mine

to sit around the dining table

and unfold

hands to lips

the open window

speaking in sun showers

a beautiful day to be a gimp

the dead cicada

like a jewel

in his palm

# 7 août

I write my aubade. To the moon
on your back. Thus

I probably
come from somewhere. Assuming
that pronouns. Are places in space.

The dilated kitchen. As everyone
takes turns. Holding
the joint to my mouth.

I leave little Latif kisses
on their fingers. And go on

into the street. Like a tribe.
The stone cathedral
necromances the sky.

He had explained it
beautifully. He likes

the subject. In the middle
of an action.

# Cratylus

You woke me up again. Cratylus.
Even with beeswax stuffed in my ear.
I could hear you howling
into the bathroom mirror. There there
Cratylus. Words can't hurt anymore.

It would have been a beautiful night
otherwise. The sky. Our carbonated etcetera.
The sky scooped into your flashing pupils.
The monosyllabic sky. Opening its mouth
as self-incrimination.

You must've been frightened
when you opened the faucet and
night came pouring out. You didn't think
it could get any weirder
than water. And now

here we are. With every faucet running. The stars getting stuck in the drain.
It's gonna be okay. At first I thought my body was a dragon. Then
a tomb. Then a way of speaking. Now. Sitting here. Next to you.
It is only an opening. You have even begun dancing. Getting each vowel
to undulate into one vibrating river. Oh yes Cratylus

everything is on fire. You were right all along. You're going to have to do
a lot more dancing. To see from up here. First. My body was a crisis. Then
an enigma. Then a liability. Now it is a brief encyclopedia. If you're confused
Cratylus. Try saying it back to yourself in a palsied accent. So that each spasm
is a word turned inside out. So that knowledge is a dyskinetic hand

quickening against your cheek.
So that when you say
your name. Nobody understands.
Oh Cratylus please.
No more crying.

No more faucets. No more bathroom
mirror. Pull each star
from the drain
and know. I can only
help by watching.

## Analysis

Things may be getting worse. The crane
for example. Against the sky. You enter

with your eyes first. Measuring things.
Before you bring in the rest of the body

strange at last. Crammed. Into the back
of the cab. Through slight adjustment

there can be slight relief. Along the river.
Parallel. The sun caught and reflected.

Waiting for your day of rest. The doctor suggests
Parkinson's medication. But first an MRI.

In which a part of you must temporarily
die. The world unhooking itself and considering

things. The security guard pushes patois
through a small metal box. Pray

fi mek your hand dem work. Dawn
adds. As she slips the egg. Into my mouth.

# 24 octobre

you didn't understand quebec
when he said to count every star

you must listen with all your might.

with each note he develops
a new cry. the long african bodysong
in which we were born.

that the world is exactly like this

there is no time to sit.
there is no time to stand.

there are only hands and feet.

yours
xadi

## 27 septembre

In this new style of suffering I adjust my flamingo feathers and take you in sharper.

This is the form I allow: you. Dots only. Dense
material.

My father holding my head. The dentist chair
ne bouge ne bouge ne. Don't move
he corrects himself. Lest I interpolate his neocolonial
rendez-vous. Where a man playing my father
translates my body. Into an incomplete sound.

Happiest day of my life. A few days ago. Since then. During. Suffering
opening
catching right in the flowerbed I made especially. For reimagining myself.
Re re re I
laugh into each thistle. A circle.

# 23 octobre

Dear Xadi

Leaning my entire left side on Saski. We swivel my right hand into the warm bird bath we had made out of the bathroom sink.

This reminds me of you. A story I heard. The one where you carry your child in your arms all the way to the Casamance. Tell me how your feet felt after days and days of walking.

Admittedly. I haven't been sitting regularly. I say I must take time but never get around to it. How did your hands feel when you finally let them open in that green water.

River child at last.

The hands are small creatures indeed.
But are they more like birds or fish.

I will sit tonight at the window with my eyes closed until I hear your answer.

## 2 mai

Each day. I am overlapping.
I am over it.
Like the moon I have been
I can see my face shimmering
against your stomach. My antistrophe
is a clay pot. My antistrophe is a black mare.

You adjust me.
It's been a pleasure. I talk to myself
clapping out the syllables. Hello moon hello
moon. Hello. I'll board a plane
and sit there for hours
looking directly into your patchwork.
This is my face. Here are my eyes.

# 24 juillet

My boy went in to get some razors.
My friend buys me a straw.

Curious bodega all at the edges. He does
a line off the screen of his phone.
The girls across the street laugh on the stoop. The shuttling
of Court Street. Of turning onto Atlantic
from the shadow of a woman who passed. And said
bout to be at the projects. Goin Hoytways.

Hold my hand while I ascend
into the summer portapotty.

Help me pull my shorts up
a little more. Remember to dissolve your ego
in the adjusting of my pockets. A few days before
I watched Mike Tyson devour a bag of mushrooms
in the middle of an interview.

Now someone is stuffing a sandwich into my face.
I call him my messiah. We always forget the napkins.

# 4 novembre

Dear Xadi

In the cab today I felt the sharp sensation of closure. What closed. Or had been closing. Or is. I am so fucking hungry. And tired of being fed. Wish they'd close me. The sharpness of it.

Instead we proceeded. Rattling along the highway. On. In. As. This is the window I look out of. Going at a rapid pace. The crippled fold of the brain as it processes. Sometimes I'd rather not.

Every lifting fork brings me a small inconceivable death. Each day the body grows. And grows and grows. My gangling little flower. What's that noise coming from in between my toes. Tell me Xadi.

Is the disability more. Like flour or rice. We're all dying to know.

# Syntax

I am not here
to accommodate you.

I shove my feet
into the metal box
I'm given
and smile.

One foot is a fish.
The other a ratbat.

This poem
is a tribal
war.

In Ogossagou
a grazing poulo
widens his jaw
until it snaps.

English
exacting her price
down the gullies
of my back.

The word crippled
lives with me
as a yapping
mawga dog.

I beat it
often.

I beat it into form.

My mother tongue.

My mother's tongue
come fi lick me.

My father tongue
hinting at the roof
of my mouth.

What is the value of $^{m}$b
or $^{ŋ}$g

# 5th & St. Marks

The summer
the saxophonist
killed me. Someone
pushed me slowly
as I spilled into the open
street. My feet
tangled in wheel.
My arms festering
in sun. This wandering
if of a man. This waxing
back like an ancient
mule. True.
Brooklyn is a dog
come lapping.
The dealer singing
on my corner. Dawn
plays her numbers.
To dance. I paw
a cracked shell of
Absolut. Sprawled out
against the sky.
Gowanus pours
across my lips.
Amanda strips
on my lift. Her bare
ass. An autonomous
design. All my life
I've been undressing
for strangers.

# Sequence

## 45C

He had been wandering along
the penises of Jimmy DeSana.
Through the trash house etc.
The door being too narrow
or too accessible for his ablebodied
friends. Or like so.

He slips himself in and out
of space. The pleasant latch
on the bathroom door for example.

The most productive time of his life
was the end. Where the diagnosed body begins.
DeSana flickers in. The flatness of it all
or. The colors. In which each picture forms
an autoimmune system. In which each picture
reminds him only of himself. And its positioning.

# 7Q

He wonders if DeSana
would mail him a photo of himself. Crippled.
Doing something ordinary in the bathroom mirror.

Brainstorming. Two spectators imagine
a technique for unevening the ass cheeks
so that the photograph would become
something. Black and white
to devour. In soft humble quantities.

What DeSana's disability sounded like before he was diagnosed.

A furry echo for example. Or the chimes of his spiked dildo.
Or as Thầy had pointed out nine years ago.

Quand vous urinez
on peut très bien faire cela en pleine conscience.

He smiles.

## 21E

Sitting back and forth. He realizes this isn't his native language.

As in.

Diamond studded gag. Reflective.

Jimmy posing in a hat or something.

The heterosexual ablebodied white suburban household.

In which whiteness becomes a dining table fetish.

Or an asexual ritual in which. The youngest male is deadpanned.

# 88B

I elevate my chair. To become an optimal spectator of jazz.

From the back of the theater where I've come to make a home.
John Zorn. A bird funneling the inside of his stomach. Into my ear.

Playing by walking on the ankles of each note. The band flamingos across. Over.

Flowerpicking the drums. Mela's snare cuts me open again. The body.
Gesticulating. This in itself. Each spasm lives a long full life. The art.

In which DeSana baseballstitches my left concavity
onto Jim Staley's trombone. The disability
its entire subjunctive mood.

# 6 février

Dear Xadi

In between the bouts of gray I'm so used to designing. I've experienced a strange
yellow. This is not like the one I find when the substances
kick in.

This yellow is far. Is of. Is in the direction.

. .

It seems I have lost the ability to perceive movement. To get a grip on light.
The people in the kitchen. Gangling. Unclear.

Like so. My morning practice continues. I want it to encroach.
I want it seeping into. People

seem to be addressing me with their words
but not. Their bodies.

No one knows what I mean when I say
the word. Body so maybe it's best. If I stop.

. .

I'll say something equivalent.

Like Doudou N'Diaye Rose. This this this. Xadi. He
presses the end of the stick into the center of his palm

And the jigéén yépp strike. The center of their drums. And sway.
Flathanded. Up and over.

Notice the color. They know exactly what I mean by this.

## 28 mai

you seem to have grown accustomed
to choreographing your periods.

choreic.
you are a million miles off.

remember the graffiti in tivaouane:
xam sa bopp.

the body dances. remembering
its many names.

translating the graffiti
you arrive first. at

know your head.
the literal translation.

the only one
you should concern yourself with.

yours
xadi

# Syntax

The sun in moving. Across the screen
he walks under. Here. Walking
is a verb that moves the subject
forward.

The Red Stripe silvers
in the shade. The chicken
place corner. Dilated.

Moving strangely forward.
The subject. Intakes the painted
swans. Where the supermarket
used to be.

He opens his mouth
for another bite.

# 10 juin

Dear Xadi

It's tiring to sit here. It's tiring not to sit here. If you wanted to sum up my life. Tired. Would cover a lot of ground.

At first I thought it was my disability.

I thought everything was due to this. My lack of drive. My shiftless quality.

My parents are afraid that if I keep going like this I will wither away.
That I will be devoured alive by my own passivity.

Passivity. The proliferation of my debilitation.

You remember that story of Siddhartha. Sitting under the tree by the river after running with those sages. After. Renunciation after. He was nothing.

But rib. Cage
and lip.

The farm girl came and gave him a bowl of rice. Then.
He was finally able to extinguish.

Passivity as the door to my disability. Which here means something strange and familiar. Like your belly button.

Xadi. When was the last time you felt your own belly button. You can tell me ... for real.

The site Xadi. Is always the body.

## 18 février

I finally cried
today. In the kitchen.

My mouth was full of bread. Sama mag
broke the plate and sunk.

Reduced to the stepping stool.

Underneath. He fled. And I.
Tried to hold it in
to my stomach. My reeling limbs.

Weeping into mom. Her arms.
Or out of. This world

white
and symmetrical.

# 24 février

He stares at the square of light sloping the branches in the bottom left corner of the painting. He is on his back either waking up or falling asleep. We cannot be sure.

On the prospect of giving up. He entertains himself. If he's going to leave the drugs. How would he maneuver in the late afternoon light.

We inspect his unshaven cheeks. He pushes us away.

This is lonely he says. The cheeks are like that because he's yet to ask. He says he's tired of asking. We wait for a long time for him to elaborate but he doesn't.

He sits up and touches our hand.

What do you make of this. He begins. This morning I was in the lift. Going up. Looking east. The sun flooded in through the metal bars. My entire vision was sun.

Then the face of my neighbor's dog. Sniffing at me through the bars.
Then sun again.

# Fingerlicked

Mingled in me the people grow toward the sky. As in today.
When we met outside. So tired.
If you put too much pepper on jerk chicken
you can't taste the jerk sauce anymore
which is how she likes it. Debating whether to get high again
I die. Quickly. The corolla is milking. Tinted yellow
as if two small fingers had smeared honey. On the underbelly of each petal.
What's new about our retrogressive metamorphosis.
In which we break ourselves. To achieve our honeykissed flora.
The sun opening at the eve of my metal footplate. You coax me
into place. By growing. My eyelashes wildflower.
I change positions. Using my legs as a single ank. I stir
the soil underneath. The sun. My prolific spleen.

## 20 mars

Dear Xadi

When they first came. I didn't even notice. Some doctors ask when they began. I clap my hands and bow. Wherever the sun comes from I come from.

In my estimation when they began they were like light. In my estimation they shot out in every direction.

I tried hating my involuntary movements. I tried loving my involuntary movements. Either way I still suffer. I go around taking more obscure and varying positions toward them. I go around and around and around like a shepherd trying to goad them into the ultimate pasture. I want to nullify. I want to jàpp. I want to gone.

No wonder why I'm all fucked up about them. I was settled on the scientific term. Which I thought I understood.

Involuntary is so far out you couldn't even see it if you caught it by the tail and dangled it in front of your face. All you'd get is the sun passing through your busy fingers.

In Latin I want and I fly are the same. That's what I miss every time I utter the word involuntary. It's the vol. The vol. The vol. I wish I could slap myself with it.

Voluntary being imbued with movement away from the center.
Involuntary existing outside of wanting. Outside of flight.

Still movement. Movement that stills.
Coming from nothing. Ending in nothing.

The sound is silent if you stop listening and hear.
The light is invisible if you stop looking and see.
The movement is still if you stop touching and feel.

## 4 novembre

this feeling. sitting
in hunger. The tathāgata ate.
that's how he got over.

my walk to thikite was like this.

nothing closing
nothing opening.

ku yàlla tàccu mu fecc.

yours
xadi

# 5 février

He wants to drink in Lac Rose so that the inside
of his stomach becomes rich  salt deposits. His ordinary shoulders.

Assuming their mansahood. He owns no body and does
not make haj. Except when he wakes up. And feels

the soles of his feet on the wooden floor. Stéphanie
is finally returning home. She takes an empty barn as a sign

of her inevitable arrival. Today. He will stay in bed
where the only eye he can identify. Is gray and shut.

Warming himself one soukou at a time. He can't really tell
what they want with him. He turns his head

in the direction of his involuntary movements
his involuntary self. Chef du village.

He considers the photo of his grandfather
again. In this one. He is fezless.

## 6 mars

Dear Xadi

We have captured something marvelous.

There I go again shitting up my words. Captured. No. Not at all.

It's as if the eyes were closed. The back of the eyes. When glass breaks the sun

into her various frequencies. A language no. A time.

Aunt Rachel said she'd pray for my flu to pass. She had to go though.

They don't let you talk on the phone during dialysis.

Dad already gave me the names of my ancestors. He emailed them to me.

Now I can't find it. That's how it be.

Weather etc. I'm on my way Xadi.

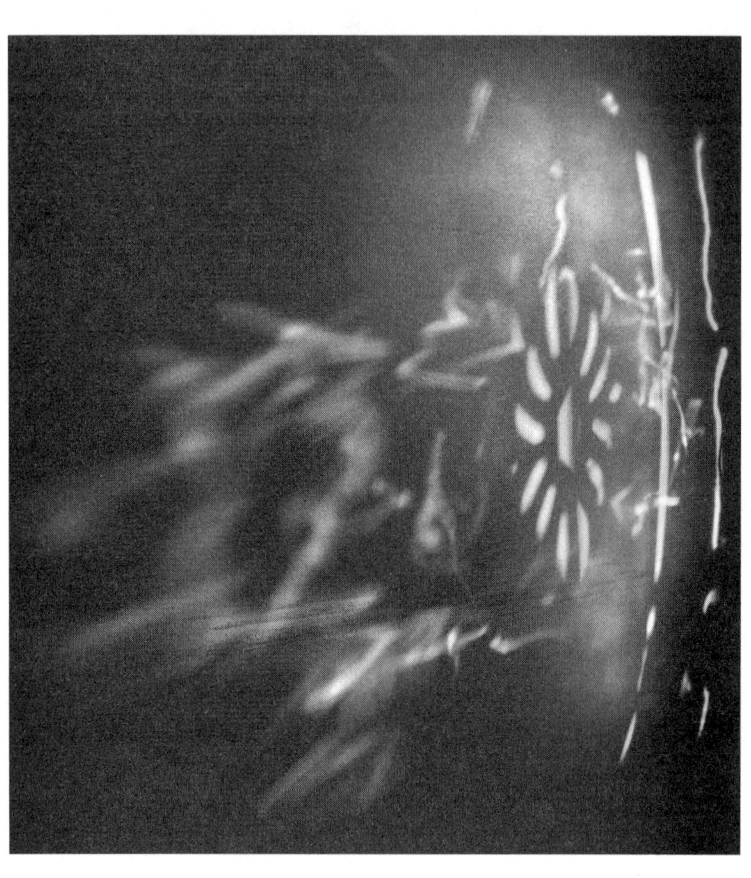

# Syntax

The thing I need now. These periods are part of my samsaric past.
To return. To be closely associated. With wheels. So that when I enter a place
people have to make room. Because there wasn't enough room
before. Do I prefer. I'm not certain. That I love my disability. Here
I is not a pronoun. But a transitive verb. And you is a preferable way.
To begin a sentence. Looking back at it. I couldn't concentrate
on my breath that night. I kept thinking of ways to make more space
for myself.

# 27 octobre

Listening to Gonsalves now. I finally understand.
Each note walking into me and opening.

The torso wrings itself into form.

Because there is no language for me. Because
I was supposed to be. Asphyxia and end.

In therapy the exercises varied

and my attitude placated. Now
I have a six-pack. And scoliosis

the music in which. I walk down Nevins

trying to find where exactly. The sentence ends.
I go among the people. Cramming all six feet of me

into the heel of my shoe.

# Analysis

Lying on his stomach again. He begins to construct a way.
Through radical reconsideration.

He takes the circumference of his disability

$$C_{dis} = 2\pi r$$

He thinks. Reaching his right hand toward the top of his bed

so that the tip of his middle finger rests. At the corner of the mattress.
So that he feels a curious stretch in his right shoulder.

He takes that to be his radius. He names it s. So that the formula now reads

$$C_{dis} = 2\pi s$$

This is a good start. Now he knows how many paces are required to round
his conditioning. He knows but he doesn't believe. So he begins.

One step. Then another. He taps against the glass perimeter.
Not thinking anymore. Just tapping. In order to get a better view.

It's hard to imagine this so he draws us a picture.
He begins with his head. Pitched silently toward the neurologist.

Who told him how lucky he was not to have an intellectual disability
as a result. Of his prenatal asphyxiation. His mouth looks like this.

He sketches a few eyes with some coordinates. He says this is the feeling
I had from the moment the doctor greeted me. That I was a child.

Though. He adds folding the paper back. I'm not sure
how much of this was me. Or him.

He begins gesticulating

wildly across the page. We aren't given much form
to align ourselves with. And we're not sure whether to mention that to him

or to sit quietly in his infantile obscurity. He senses this.

And the gesticulations become more disorienting. Layered.
Junglelike. Entirely out of the neurologist's line of sight. He stops.

And places the paper neatly at our feet. It is slightly crumpled

from the spasms. He waits until we've considered the artifact.
In its context and framing. Then adds almost ducklike.

I was going to take his stupid medicine and his little MRI
even after he had called me a puzzle. A mystery. His guinea.

Pig. He stomps on the paper. He stomps on the paper.

He stomps on the paper. We see him.

# Aubade

In the night I am sorry. The curtains glow. I stand still
like a blowing dress. Everyone wants to eat me.
Until the center of my heart is round and glassy.

In life I was complacent. And there's nothing worse
than nudging a muscular calf with the tip of your nose.
They want to peel me open and drain me into the belly

of a star. And what is worse. This night. I am lying on my back.
A current. Powered by broken things. The light through my window
thickening. Tomorrow will come. And I will mistake it. Again. For morning.

# Foreword

I began this practice over a year ago. Of only using periods to write poetry.

In the following snapshots of this practice. I invite you into my body.
Your body. The disability. The intake of the world.

This practice is not mine. This disability is not mine. It is ours.

You feed me for example. Aiming skillfully or unskillfully
at my moving mouth.

Sometimes I knock the spoon over. The rice gets everywhere.
And you get frustrated.
Sometimes I knock the spoon. Over. The rice gets everywhere
and I get. Frustrated.
Sometimes. I knock the spoon over. The rice gets everywhere
and. We laugh.

This practice doesn't ameliorate. Deal with. Address.
Or get at the disability. This practice
is our exhabilitation. It doesn't blind the ablebodied eye.
It doesn't deafen the ablebodied ear. It doesn't
numb the ablebodied tongue. It doesn't palsy the ablebodied fingers.
And it doesn't queer the ablebodied thought.

This practice occurs beyond the able body.

The choreic period begins and ends with the body. Qua body.

This practice exists exenglish. Exhabilis. Exhabēre.
Never to have a disability.
Never to have a disorder.
Never to have a condition.

I want you to join me in the practice of not having. With every period. We relinquish the things that we have. And mark the thing that we do. The thing that we be.

I do the disability good. I disable and laugh. I am big suffering. I cripple forward into bed. I become the verb you have yet to name.

We begin always with the period. Not just at the end of the sentence where it is often ghettoed. But in the beginning. In the middle. Along the sides. On top of. The períodos rounding and rounding. Until its sentence is the open wound it leaves behind. It slips into.

This practice keeps me. So that I can tell you the name of my disability like the name of an old friend.

Please meet Scoliosis. Please meet Athetosis. Please meet Chorea.
Please meet cannot sleep some nights and each position taken up
is budding into my unique deterioration.

With each period I hand you my disability. Can you hold it without having. Can you touch it without grasping. Can you know it without understanding.

# 24 janvier

A square of light on the black bed.

Thirty reps.

He has forgotten himself.

# Notes

The epistolary poems are inspired by the letters in *Dropping Ashes on the Buddha* between Zen master Seung Sahn and his students. I discovered this book thanks to my dear friend, poet, and dhamma brother—Wil Wynn.

"3 octobre" is dedicated to my home attendant and friend, Cruz. The lyric "Vivo trabajaaaando" is from "Porque Te Fuiste" by Anthony Santos.

"Djabote" is an ekphrastic poem after the album *Djabote* by Doudou N'Diaye Rose where each stanza in the poem corresponds to a song in their respective order. This poem was also in conversation with the live performance of the album, shot on Gorée Island.

"9 novembre" is dedicated to Declan and Mark, who were counselors at the summer camp I went to: the Southampton Fresh Air Home. It's also dedicated to Mark Borczon, a poet and friend.

"At Stop & Shop," "Analysis," and "5th and St. Marks" are dedicated to Dawn, my former home attendant and friend who taught me a lot about reggae.

"12 février" is dedicated to my former home attendant and friend Sandra.

"3 juillet" was written while I was visiting my friend, Colleen, in Harrisburg.

"Cratylus" is named after and written in conversation with the Platonic dialogue.

"24 octobre" is dedicated to the saxophonist Ike Quebec.

"23 octobre" is dedicated to my friends and dear poets Saski Erickson Weisbrod and Liv Waite.

"24 juillet" is dedicated to my friend and poet Andres Cordoba.

"Sequence" was written in response to *Jimmy DeSana: Submission*, an exhibit at the Brooklyn Museum. In Section 7Q, the lines "Quand vous urinez / on peut très bien faire cela en pleine conscience" were spoken by Thich Nhat Hanh during a dharma talk. It was uploaded to YouTube under the name "Retraite Francophone | Thich Nhat Hanh, 2013.03.17." And in Section 88B, I'm responding to a concert I went to after the exhibit called "IMPROV NIGHTS – A Tribute to Derek Bailey" at Roulette Intermedium.

"5 février" is dedicated to my friend Stéphanie Fribourg.

"27 octobre" is dedicated to the saxophonist Paul Gonsalves.

# Acknowledgments

I first want to thank my dear friend and fellow poet, John Lee Clark, who introduced me to the poet and editor Chris Martin. It warms my heart that this book came into existence through the communion of disabled poets. I'm so honored and thankful to Chris for welcoming me into the Multiverse family, where my poetry feels completely at home.

The poems in this book dance along with the poems of Adam Wolfond, Hannah Emerson, JJJJJerome Ellis, Imane Boukaila, Lauren Russell, and all the future poets who will contribute to this neuroqueer, mad, nonspeaking, disfluent, choreic chorus.

The concept for this book came from B.K. Fischer's course called The Comma Sutra, which was one of the most formative classes I took as an MFA student. Thank you B.K. for encouraging me to think deeply about these small mysterious marks we put between our letters!

I also want to thank my professors Alan Gilbert, Mark Bibbins, Jay Deshpande, Susan Bernofsky, Edwin Torres, Cynthia Cruz, Joshua Edwards, Dorothea Lasky, Timothy Donnelly and Jeremy Tiang for helping me in various ways to create and assemble this collection of poetry.

This book would not have been possible without the love and generous support of my friends Saski Erikson Weisbrod, Ally Shilson, Dylan Gilbert, Liv Waite, Sumayyah Smith, Damien McClendon, j. eunsun, Kyle Hurysz, Loisa Fenichell, Addison Schoeman, Rose DeMaris, Colleen O'Neal, Ryan Patrick Cook, Kellie Diodato, Andres Cordoba, and Kai Lilly Karpman.

I'm also incredibly grateful to my parents and brothers for all their love, care, and encouragement. They are the true authors of my poetry.

And finally, I give many thanks and praises to the following journals where these poems appear:

*Poetry*: "6 février," "7 août," "Cratylus," and "Syntax" ("The thing I need now . . .")
*Poem-A-Day*: "Douglass Pool"
*Pastel Serenity*: "2 mai"
*Epiphany*: "24 juillet" and "At Stop & Shop" ("Two ripe plátanos . . .")

LATIF ASKIA BA is a poet with Choreic Cerebral Palsy from Brooklyn, New York. He received his MFA in Creative Writing from Columbia University and was the Print Poetry Editor for the *Columbia Journal*'s sixty-first issue. He is the author *The Machine Code of a Bleeding Moon*, and his work appears in *Poetry* magazine and many other publications.

multiverse

Multiverse is a literary series devoted to different ways of languaging. It primarily emerges from the practices and creativity of neurodivergent, autistic, neuroqueer, mad, nonspeaking, and disabled cultures. The desire of Multiverse is to serially surface multiple universes of underheard language that might intersect, resonate, and aggregate toward liberatory futures. In other words, each book in the Multiverse series gestures toward a correspondence—human and more-than-human—that lovingly exceeds what is normal and normative in our society, questioning and augmenting what literary culture is, has been, and can be.

Founded as a nonprofit organization in 1980, Milkweed Editions is an independent publisher. Our mission is to identify, nurture, and publish transformative literature, and build an engaged community around it.

We are based in Bdé Óta Othúŋwe (Minneapolis) in Mní Sota Makhóčhe (Minnesota), the traditional homeland of the Dakhóta and Anishinaabe (Ojibwe) people and current home to many thousands of Dakhóta, Ojibwe, and other Indigenous people, including four federally recognized Dakhóta nations and seven federally recognized Ojibwe nations.

We believe all flourishing is mutual, and we envision a future in which all can thrive. Realizing such a vision requires reflection on historical legacies and engagement with current realities. We humbly encourage readers to do the same.

milkweed.org

Milkweed Editions, an independent nonprofit literary publisher, gratefully acknowledges sustaining support from our board of directors, the McKnight Foundation, the National Endowment for the Arts, and many generous contributions from foundations, corporations, and thousands of individuals—our readers. This activity is made possible by the voters of Minnesota through a Minnesota State Arts Board Operating Support grant, thanks to a legislative appropriation from the Arts and Cultural Heritage Fund.

Interior design by Tijqua Daiker
Typeset in Vendetta

Vendetta was designed in 1999 by John Downer for the Emigre type foundry. The design of Vendetta was influenced by the design of types by Roman punchcutters who traced their aesthetic lineage to Nicolas Jenson's seminal 1470 text *De Evangelica Praeparatione*, a work of Christian apologetics written in the 4th century AD by the historian Eusebius.